LAW FOR CHILDREN

VOLUME 2, ISSUE 1 OF BRAIN BOOSTER ARTICLES

FURQUAN AHMAD

Contents

Preface

"Start writing, no matter what. The water does not flow until the faucet is turned on".

- Louis L'Amour

Hundreds of students and professors are contributing their work to Brain Booster Articles, we are here to provide ample information about Law and Contemporary issues. Our aim is to provide a platform for today's generation to express their views and ideas on law and contemporary law.

Publication

This research paper is published in volume 2, issue 1 of Brain Booster Articles

Author

Furquan Ahmad

CHAPTER ONE

Abstract

A child is regarded as an important national asset as the future of any nation depends on how its children mature and develop. Nowadays the protection of children from all forms of exploitation and abuse has become a major goal of our society. There have been many cases of child abuse in the form of sexual abuse, child marriage, infant breastfeeding, verbal abuse, child abuse, prostitution, child pornography and child abuse that indirectly highlight the failure of our society to protect our future generations. Child protection is considered a major responsibility of government as well as society and the challenges and problems children face are taken into account. In this paper we have specifically addressed the various forms of violence against children and included a case study, local laws and a children's rights proposal in India.

CHAPTER TWO

Introduction

The question of children's rights has arisen as one of the most intriguing issues discussed in the new millennium. The fact is that even today children are part of a small group that has been denied so far about the realization of human rights and social justice. The main reason for this is that children are not yet fully formed in the true sense of the word. Besides, they are often unable to defend themselves physically, mentally, and economically. In this rapidly changing era of globalization, care for the right of the child at all levels has taken its toll. This affects not only the entire pricing system, but also their current social and economic needs. There is no doubt that the future of humanity depends largely on children, even when an incomplete and careless approach has been taken to bring them into the normal social and political order.

This discrimination becomes even more serious when a child is orphaned, lonely, homeless, homeless, child laborer, incarcerated, domestic worker, street child, physically or mentally disabled child. In such cases, they remain in a state of neglect and are at greater risk for the crimes committed against them. Violations of Children's Rights are linked to social ills. From real crime to child neglect and child rearing, innocence, ignorance, poor exposure, improper care, lack of proper guidance and a lack of a good social security system are some of the major reasons for continuing to be vulnerable to child abuse.

CHAPTER THREE

Legal Child Definition

The word 'Child' is not defined in the Constitution of India. According to Article 1 of the United Nations Convention on the Rights of the Child 1989, 'a child means every person under the age of eighteen unless, under the law applicable to a child, the majority is found prematurely'3. The legal definition of a child usually depends on the purpose. There are many laws in India that define the word 'Child' depending on the purpose. Under the Indian Planting Act, 1875 is 18 years old and in the case of a child nominated by a person and his or her place of caregiver or place is under the direction of the Ward Court of twenty-one years.

Under the Child Abuse (Prevention and Control) Act, 1986, a child means a person under the age of fourteen years. Under the Prevention of Child Marriage Act, 1926, a child means a person who, if a man, has not attained the age of twenty-one years and, if a woman, has not attained the age of eighteen years. Under the Child Justice Act (Care and Protection), 2000, 'Child' or 'Child' means a person under the age of eighteen years.

United Nations Convention on the Rights of the Child (CRC) The United Nations Convention on the Rights of the Child (UNCRC) is a comprehensive, international commitment on the rights of children, adopted by the UN General Assembly in 1989. We include children's social and political rights (such as their rule of law), social, economic and cultural rights (such as adequate living conditions) and protection rights (from abuse and exploitation). The child is described at the UNCRC as a person under the age of 18.

Children are God's greatest gift to man, our most precious possession. The well-being and development of any community depends largely on the health and well-being of their children. It has been said that 'the one who holds the souls of children in charge of the nation'.4 The physical and mental health of a nation is largely determined by the way we were formed in the beginning. Justice V.R. Krishna Iyer states that it is our responsibility in this generation to create every opportunity for every child to express his or her personality and to reach his or her full potential physically, morally, mentally and spiritually and it is the birthright of every child who cries for justice worldwide.

During World War II Winston Churchill stated that "there is no better investment in any society than milking children." This petition to the people everywhere, this fundamental belief in Juvenile Justice, this reorganization of the number of unborn children, is the beginning of Juvenile Justice, said Justice Krishna Iyer.

Big Problems of Children in India

- Child labor.
- Girl Child.
- Malnutrition.
- Poverty.
- Uneducation.
- Child Marriage.
- Child Trafficking.
- Gender inequality.

CHAPTER FOUR

Constitutional Provisions Relating to Children

The founders of our Constitution are known for the fact that national development can be achieved through the development of the children of the nation and it is necessary to protect children from exploitation.

The following are the provisions of the Indian Constitution concerning children:

Constitutional guarantees specifically for children include

Section 21A provides that the State will provide free and compulsory education to all children between the ages of six and fourteen as the State may determine.

Section 24 provides that no child under the age of fourteen may be employed to work in any industry or mine or to engage in any other dangerous occupation.

Section 39 (e) provides that, in particular, it will direct its policy on ensuring that the health and capacity of workers, men and women, and the age of children are not violated and that citizens are not compelled by economic necessity. avocations that do not correspond to their age or strength.

Section 39 (f) provides that, in particular, it will guide its policy in ensuring that children are provided with opportunities and resources to grow up healthy and under conditions of freedom and dignity and that childhood and youth are protected from exploitation and morality. and material waste.

Section 45 provides that the State shall endeavor to provide early childhood care and education for all children up to the age of six years.

In addition, Children have the same rights as equal citizens of India, as with any other adult male or female:

Article 14 provides that the State may not forbid any person to be equal before the law or equal protection of the laws in the territory of India.

Article 15 The right to discrimination

Article 21 provides that no one shall be arbitrarily deprived of his nationality nor denied the right to change his nationality.

Article 23 The right to be protected from trafficking and to forced labor.

Article 29 The right of young people to protect their interests.

Article 46 The right of vulnerable classes to be protected from social injustice and all forms of exploitation.

Article 47 The right to good nutrition and quality of life and to the welfare of the community.

Other Rules

Apart from the Constitution there are a lot of laws that affect children. The following are some of them:

The Children (Pledging of Labor) Act, 1933

The law was enacted in the pre-independence era but is still in force. The purpose of the Act is to eliminate malpractice from child labor undertaking. An agreement to guarantee child labor under the age of 15 by a parent or guardian as compensation for any payment or benefit is invalid.8, the Act punishes both parent or guardian and employer in the event of child labor. The employer is liable to pay a fine of Rs.200 / - 9 and the parent or guardian is liable to pay a fine of up to Rs.50 / - /

Child Labor Act, 1938

This is the first non-repeal rule in the legal code that regulates the employment of people under the age of certain occupation. Provides: No child under the age of 15 may be employed in any activity related to the transport of passengers, goods or postal trains, or a port official within the boundaries of the port12. Limited protection for children between the ages of 15-17. This protection does not apply to children who are employed as students or who receive internships.

Industrial Act, 1948

The first Welfare Act passed by the British was the Factories Act, 1881. Implementation of the Act was restricted: The Act was amended in 1948 with the keys

The features are as follows Preventing the employment of children under the age of 14 in factory14. The factory oversees the establishment, which employs 10 or more workers with the help of energy or 20 or more employees without the assistance of energy15. Persons between the ages of 14 and 15, may be employed under the following restrictions provided under Sections 68, 69 and 71 of the Act: Such persons must have a competency certificate issued by a surgeon and must carry a reference token. certificate.16 # Certified Surgeon should follow the procedure set out in Section 69. # They must not work at night that is 12 consecutive hours including the time from 10 PM to 6 AM.

Mining Act, 1952

The scope of the Mines Act is limited. It applies to excavations where work is done for the purpose of searching for or extracting minerals or being done.19 It not only restricts the employment of any 'child' 20 but even the presence of a child in any part of an underground mine or area. any active open cast in which mining operations are carried out.21 A young woman over the age of sixteen is allowed to work only if she has a doctor's certificate of competency.22 The certificate is valid for 12 months only.

Apprentice Act, 1961

The purpose of this Act is to provide for the regulation and management of apprenticeships training in trade and related matters. No one is eligible to join as a student for vocational training unless they have completed 14 years of age and meet other levels of physical fitness and education as may be determined. When a student is young his or her caregiver needs to enter into a study contract with the employer and will be registered with the Learning Advisor.

CHAPTER FIVE

Child Use Act (Prevention and Control), 1986

The law is the result of various recommendations made by a series of Committees.26 While there was an ongoing need to adopt the same broader law prohibiting the participation of children in other activities to achieve this goal, parliament enacted the Child Use (Prevention) Act. and Regulation), 1986

(CLPRA) came into effect on 23 December 1986. The objectives of the Child Use (Prevention and Control) Act of 1986 are:

- Prohibition of child labor which means those under the age of fourteen, in certain occupations and processes.
- Establish procedures for determining the modification of a restricted activity plan or procedures.
- Controlling working conditions for employed children when they are not prohibited from working.
- Lowering advanced child labor penalties in contravention of the provisions of this Act and other laws prohibiting child labor.

Baby Breastfeeding, Bottle Feeding and Baby Feeding Act (Production, Supply and Distribution Act) 1992

The Act regulates the production, supply and distribution of infant formula, breastfeeding bottles and infant formulas for the protection and promotion of breastfeeding and to ensure the proper use of infant formula and other emerging issues.

The Pre-Natal Diagnostic Technique (Regulation and Prevention of Abuse) Act 1994

The Act provides for the use of prenatal diagnostic methods for the purpose of determining genetic or metabolic or chromosomal abnormalities or certain birth defects or sexual disorders and to prevent the misuse of such procedures for premature purposes. -prepare sexual reproduction leading to female fetal.

Child Justice (Child Care and Protection) Act, 2000

This Act applies to the law relating to children in conflict with the law and to children in need of care and protection, by providing appropriate care, protection and treatment to meet their developmental needs and by using the best approach for children in judging and resolving problems. matters that benefit children and their eventual rehabilitation through the various institutions established under the Act.

Right to Education (RTE) Act, 2009

Free and compulsory education for all Indian children aged 6 to 14 years. No child shall be deprived of, terminated or required to pass a board examination until he or she has completed elementary education. If a child over the age of 6 is not admitted to any school or has not been able to complete his or her primary education, it means that he or she will be admitted to a class that is the same age. However, if the case may be that the child is admitted directly to a class appropriate for his or her age, then, in order to fit others, he or she will be entitled to specialized training within those time limits that may be determined. Provided that such a child is entitled to a basic education shall be entitled to a free education until he or she completes primary education even after 14 years.

Proof of age of admission: For the purpose of admission to a basic education, the child's age will be determined on the basis of a birth certificate issued in accordance with the Birth Benefits. Registration of Bodies and Marriages Act 1856, or on the basis of that document may be prescribed. No child will be denied admission to school due to lack of proof of age. A child who completes primary school will be awarded a certificate. The call needs to be taken at a fixed level for student and teacher. Improving the quality of education is important.

Government policies regarding children

The Government of India has made many policies regarding the physical, mental and social development of the country's children.30 The government has also made many policies for the health and education of children. The following are some of the key Government policies on children:

- National Children's Policy, 1974.
- National Education Policy, 1986.
- National Child Employment Policy, 1987.
- National Health Policy, 2002.
- National Children's Policy 1974

India is one of the few countries in the world with a written policy for children. This policy declares that children are 'the property of the highest order'.31 The following are some of the features of the policy:

- All children will be covered under a comprehensive health plan.
- Programs that will be implemented to provide children with nutritious food and eliminate malnutrition in children.
- Provide illegal education.
- Special care to be taken for children with physical, mental disabilities.32
- All children will be guaranteed equal opportunities.

National Education Policy 1986

This was the second policy on education; the first policy of 1968 was reviewed by this policy. This policy has been considered historic. This policy has given significant impetus to International Primary Education. It also gave importance to early childhood care and education. It emphasized the need for greater investment in the development of The Rights Of Children in India through Government and voluntary organizations. Later many programs were made across the country such as Operation Black Board, Sarva Siksha An etc. Operation Black Board and Sarva Siksha Abhiyan became very popular throughout the country.

National Child Labor Policy 1987

The National Policy on Child Employment is a landmark initiative in the ongoing eradication of child labor in India. The policy includes actions in the areas of education, health, nutrition, integrated child development and employment.

The National Child Employment Policy is under the following three headings:

- Legal System.
- Focus on general child benefit programs wherever possible.

A project-based app in the most densely populated areas of child labor / wages.

National Health Policy of 2002

The first health policy, 1983 aimed at achieving 'universal health by the year 2000'. The second health policy, 2002 aims to prioritize health problems in schools aimed at health education and regular school health check-ups. A key element of this policy was to prevent communicable diseases such as HIV / AIDS and to provide childhood immunizations against all major preventable diseases.

<u>**Response from Judicial**</u>

M.C. Mehta Vs. Tamil Nadu District and others

In this case, the plaintiff of Indian activist M.C. Mehta sued the state of Tamil Nadu for improving the working conditions of children and for providing rescued children with hazardous jobs through education. The Supreme Court has issued a landmark decision stating that the Indian Constitution (Article 24) requires the state to strive to provide free, compulsory education for children. The Court found that children under the age of 14 could not work at risk, and ordered the government to establish and maintain a child welfare fund. Employers who have violated child labor laws will be required to deposit money into a fund; the government will also be required to provide a parent of each child involved in hazardous work, or to make a deposit in the fund.

Bandhua Mukti Morcha Vs. Union of India and others

In this case, the Supreme Court stated, "Therefore, whenever it is determined that an employee is required to perform a compulsory service, the Court will suggest that he or she be required to do so in advance of the foreclosure or other economic considerations obtained by him or her. and, therefore, is a bound employee.This consideration may be challenged by the employer and the State Government if they choose but unless and until provided that the dismissal of this consideration is provided, the Court must proceed on the basis that the employee is a detained employee entitled to benefit from the provisions of the Act. The State Government may not relinquish its obligation to identify, release and rehabilitate detained employees on the grounds that while the affected employees may provide compulsory labor, the State Government has no obligation to them except to demonstrate appropriate legal action in accordance with the rules of the justice system.

J.P.Unnikrishnan & Others Vs. Andhra Pradesh Region & others

In this case, the Supreme Court ruled that the citizens of this country have a fundamental right to education and that this right comes from Article 21 of the Constitution. This right, however, is not a complete right. Every child / citizen in this country is entitled to free education until the age of fourteen. Thereafter, his right to education is subject to the limits of economic power and development of the State.

Mohini Jain vs. State of Karnataka

In this regard, the Supreme Court was called upon to address the issue of the right to education under Article 41 and the Court reaffirmed the importance of the Guidelines by holding that the right to education is in line with Fundamental Rights and made the following: Note: These principles must be submitted to the Fundamental Rights. Both are additions to each other. The State is subject to the constitutional mandate of each other. The State is subject to the statutory mandate to create conditions in which the Fundamental Rights guaranteed to the people under Part III may be enjoyed by all. Without making the "Right to Education" under Article 41 of the Constitution real, the Fundamental Rights under Chapter III will remain inaccessible to the majority of the illiterate. The fundamental rights guaranteed under Part III of the Constitution of India which include the right to freedom of speech and expression and other rights under Article 19 cannot be fully realized and fully enjoyed unless a citizen is educated and recognizes his or her individual dignity ".

Vishal Jeet vs. Union of India

The H'onble Supreme Court has issued directives to the national government to establish homes for the rehabilitation of street children and young girls who have been pushed into the 'meat trade' in secure housing. "

Gaurav Jain vs. Union of India

The H'onble Supreme Court will rehabilitate children and child prostitutes after extensive research of the matter .In addition, children's homes should be used for child prostitution rehabilitation.

People's Union Democratic Reforms vs. Union of India (Asian Case)

Justice PNBhagwati, (1) Begar defines compulsory labor without pay (2) Non-payment of minimum wages comes by force of compulsory labor. (3) but also power arises as a result of forced economic conditions, which leave no other option for the needy and compel him to provide a service or service even though earnings are less than the minimum wage. (4) Articles 17,23 and 24 may also be enforced on private individuals. In this case it is the constitutional obligation of the state to provide protection. (5)

Construction activities are dangerous .So the employment of a child under the age of 14 in construction work is a violation of Section 24.

Sanjit Roy vs. State of Rajasthan

Justice, P.N.Bhagwati, Employees were working with the Department of Public Works, Rajasthan and could not be paid less. The court ruled that non-payment of minimum wage was subject to compulsory labor. Justice P.N.Bhagwati, "The state cannot be allowed to exploit the disadvantages of the affected people and to render services or services to them when you pay less than the minimum wage. No practical, useful work can be allowed to build upon the blood and sweat of people who are reduced to nothingness because of drought and deprivation. "

Neeraja Chaudhary vs. State of Madhya Pradesh

Justice P.N. Bhagwati, "Whenever it is found that any employee is obliged to provide a service without pay or remuneration, it is presumed that he or she is a bound employee unless the employer or the State Government disputes separate evidence for dismissing that consideration. "The Court emphasized the release and reinstatement of the imprisoned workers.

State of Gujarat vs. Hon'ble High Court of Gujarat

All types of prisoners, including those sentenced to life imprisonment, will be entitled to a minimum wage. Otherwise, it could be a beggar.

Staff Working in Salal Hydro-Project vs State of Jammu & Kashmir

Justice P.N.Bhagwati The same building projects are dangerous. Therefore the employment of a child under the age of 14 in construction activities violates Article 24 article.

CHAPTER SIX

Conclusion and Suggestion

Children build important human resources for the nation. The future of a nation depends on how its children grow and develop. The famous poet Milton said Child Shows the man as the morning marks the day. It is therefore the duty of the community to care for every child with the aim of ensuring the full development of his or her personality. Children are the future guardians and trustees of the Society: they are the messengers of our knowledge, cultural heritage, ideas and philosophies. Children are the realities of the future such as great teachers, scientists, judges, governors, doctors, editors, engineers, politicians by whom the whole society was established (rest). Unfortunately millions of children are deprived of their childhood and the right to education and as a result are exploited and abused.46

Suggestions

- The current theme of the Child Labor (Prevention and Control) Act of 1986 should be amended as the Child Labor (Prevention and Rehabilitation) Act, to focus more on rehabilitation rather than control.
- Every provincial government will draft the Laws under the Education Rights Act, 2009 as soon as possible in order to give effect to the provisions of the Act.
- The Government of India must ratify Convention No. 182 and Recommendation No.190 relating to the "Prohibition and Immediate Action on the Elimination of Child Abuse". The Convention was adopted in 1999 but has not yet been ratified by the Government.
- Child labor in any other occupation involving the Agriculture / Farming sector should be considered a tangible, non-bailable and non-binding offense.

- Government should encourage NGOs to end child labor by providing appropriate budgets from time to time and accountability should focus on NGOs to ensure that funds are used for the intended purpose.
- The Judiciary should be more proactive in handling child labor cases. The general rule of 'doubtful profit' cannot be given to offending employers. When found guilty, the employer must be punished with imprisonment and not fined. In the case of punishment, the penalty for imprisonment should be made a common law and the imposition of a fine should be different. This discourages employers. In addition there is a need to increase the sentencing rate.